My Gentle Butterfly

Dr. Claus

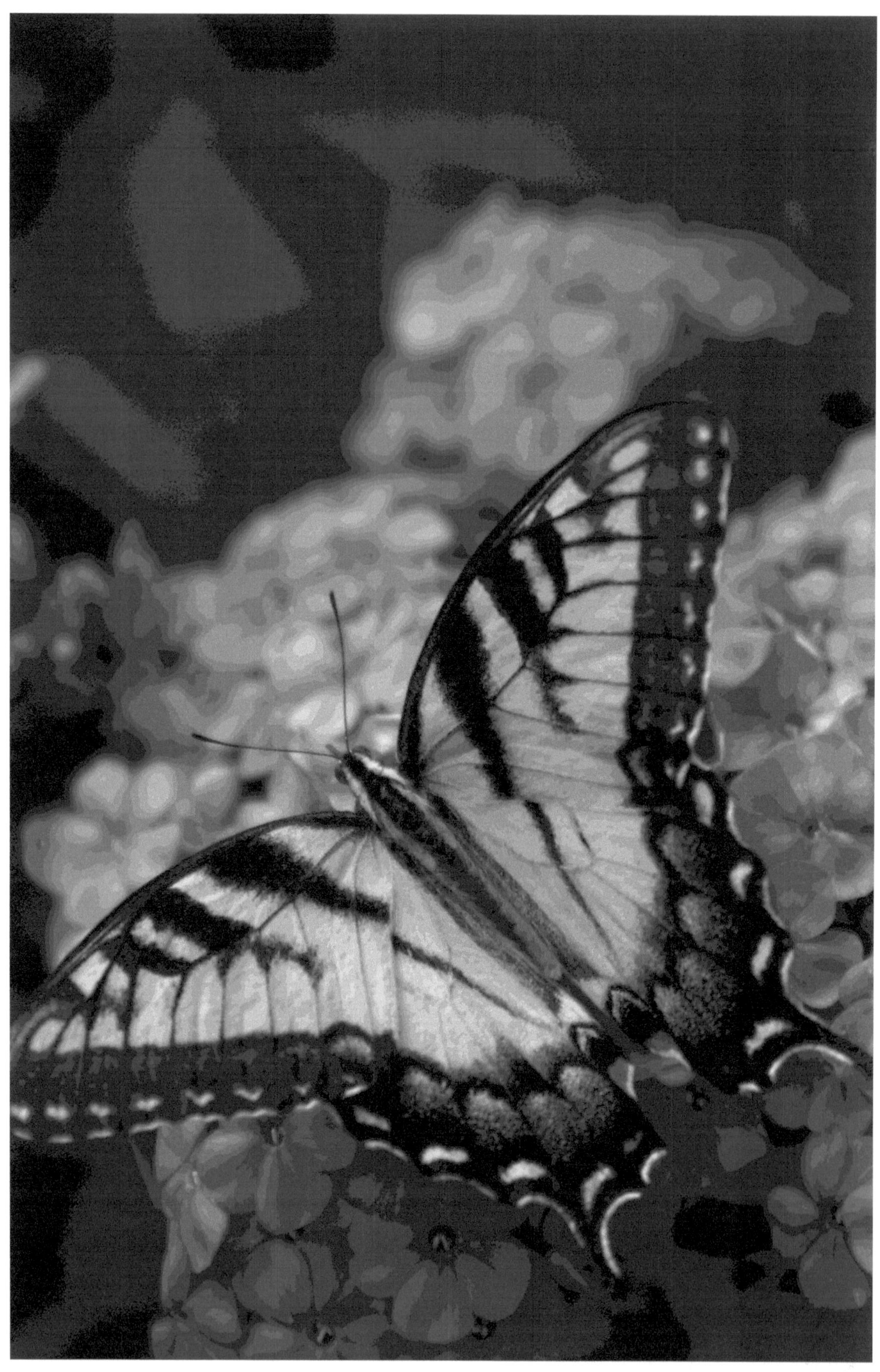

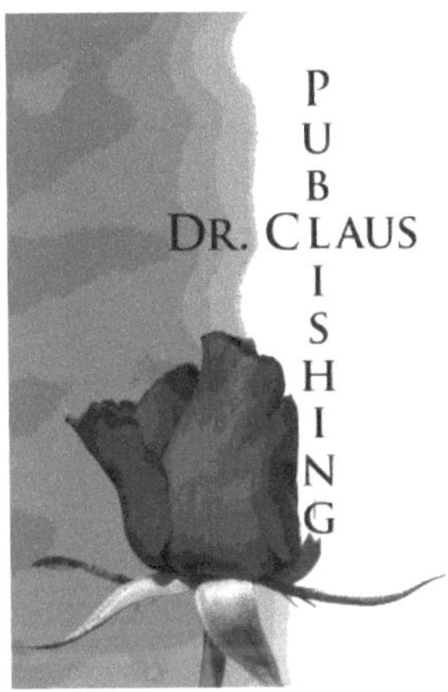

PUBLISHED BY DR. CLAUS PUBLISHING

First Edition

ISBN: 1-61497-014-9

ISBN-13: 978-1-61497-014-9

Library of Congress Control Number: 2011917752

DEDICATION

Nicole

CONTENTS

ACKNOWLEDGMENT

During the war, my heart of stone was taken from my chest.
In place of that stone, I received a heart of flesh.
My old heart was handed back to me and as I received this heart of stone,
my thumbprint was forever seared into this rock.
I carry this heart of stone with me wherever I may go.
On any given day when words of doubt rain down upon my soul,
I reach for a stone once embedded in my chest
and I place my thumb into the mark.

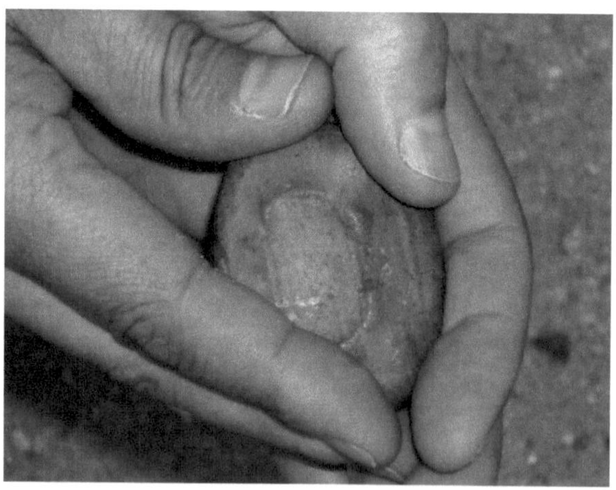

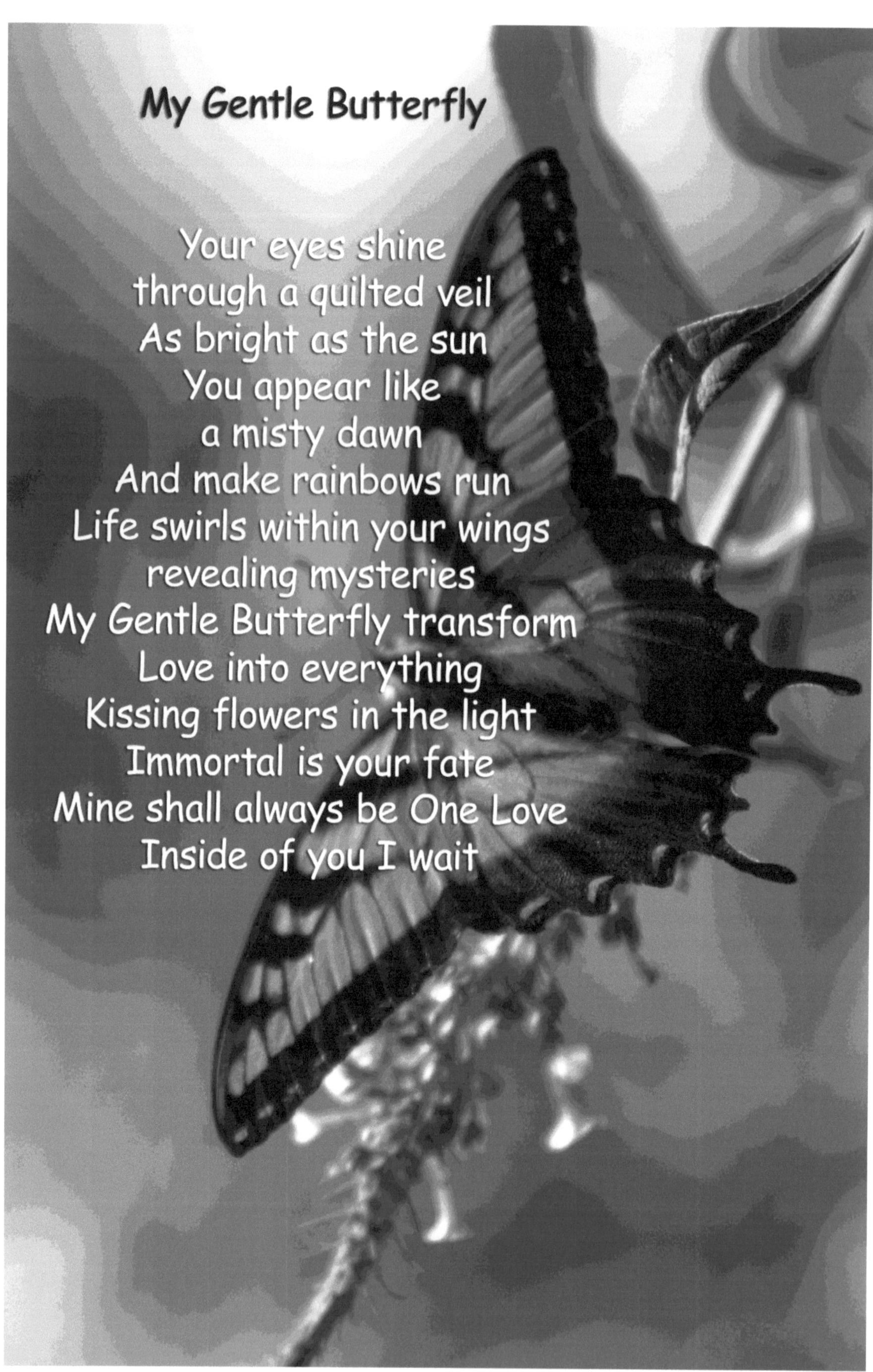
My Gentle Butterfly
Your eyes shine
through a quilted veil
As bright as the sun
You appear like
a misty dawn
And make rainbows run
Life swirls within your wings
revealing mysteries
My Gentle Butterfly transform
Love into everything
Kissing flowers in the light
Immortal is your fate
Mine shall always be One Love
Inside of you I wait

My Lover

You are radiant like the sun
Outstanding among thousands
Your head is purest gold
Your hair is wavy
Your eyes are like doves
by gently flowing water
washed in milk
and mounted like jewels
Your cheeks are like
beds of spices
Your lips are like lilies
dripping with Love
I taste you
How beautiful you are
And how pleasing
My Lover
With your delights

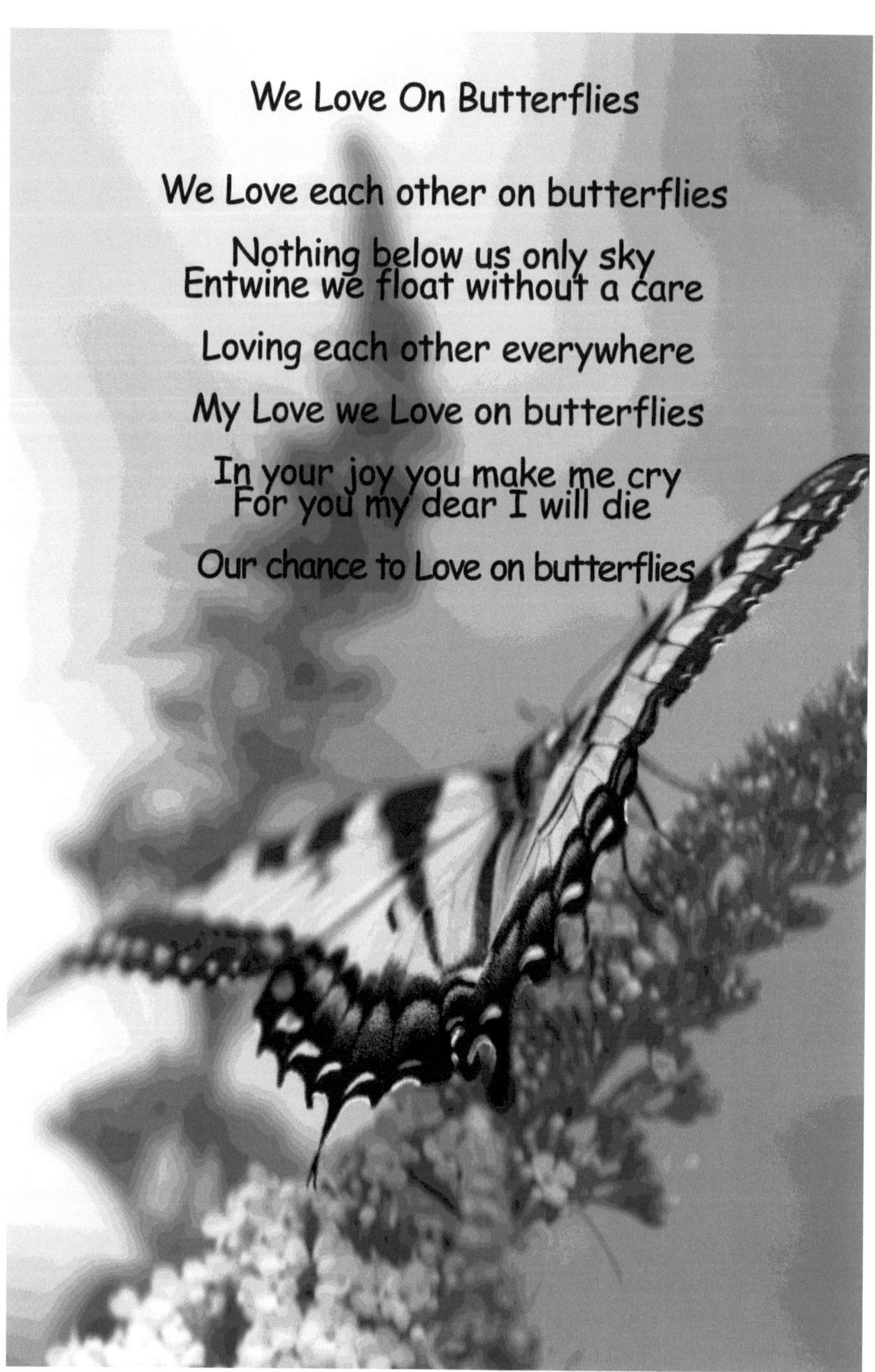
We Love On Butterflies
We Love each other on butterflies
Nothing below us only sky
Entwine we float without a care
Loving each other everywhere
My Love we Love on butterflies
In your joy you make me cry
For you my dear I will die
Our chance to Love on butterflies

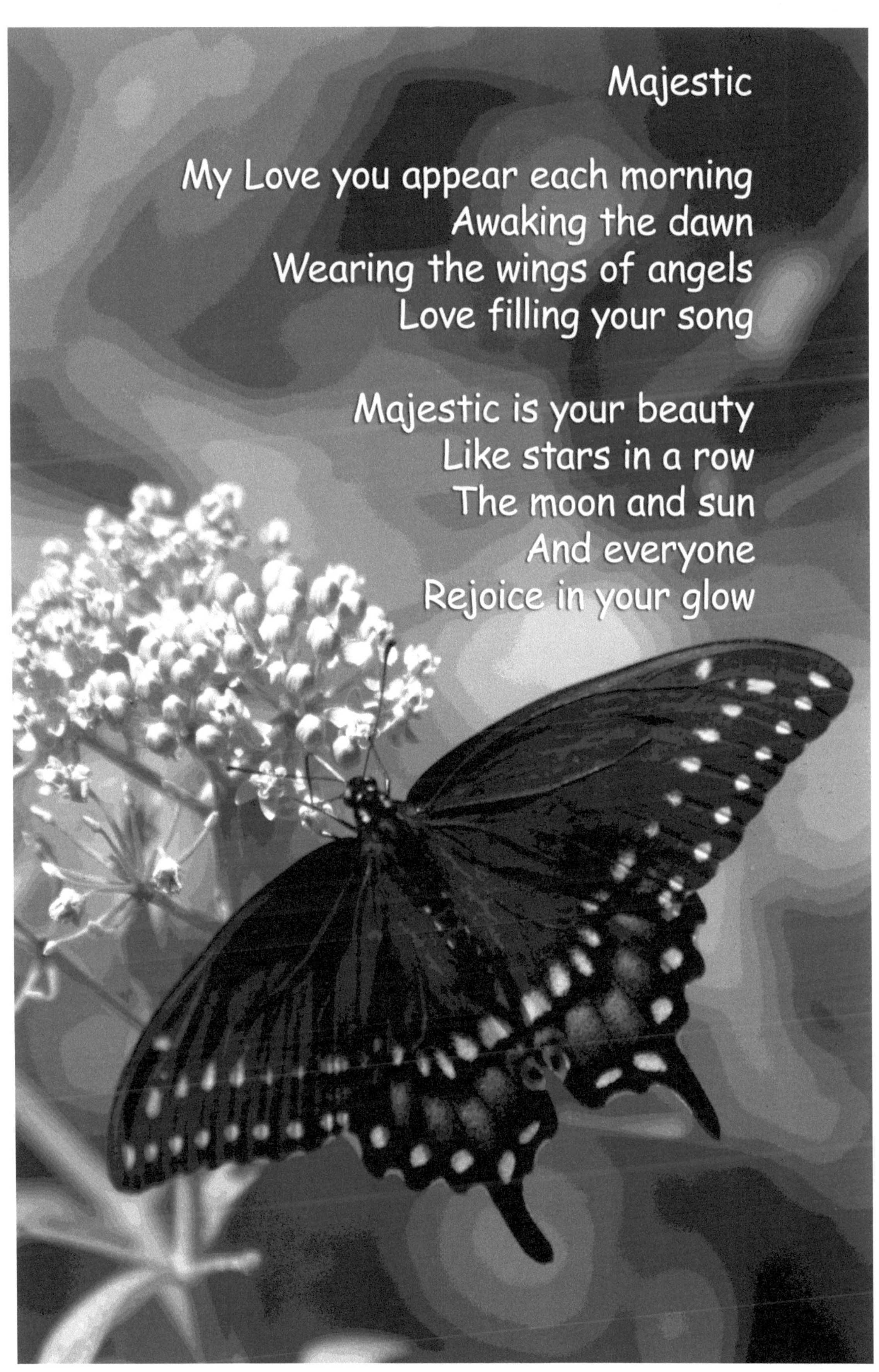
Majestic

My Love you appear each morning
Awaking the dawn
Wearing the wings of angels
Love filling your song

Majestic is your beauty
Like stars in a row
The moon and sun
And everyone
Rejoice in your glow

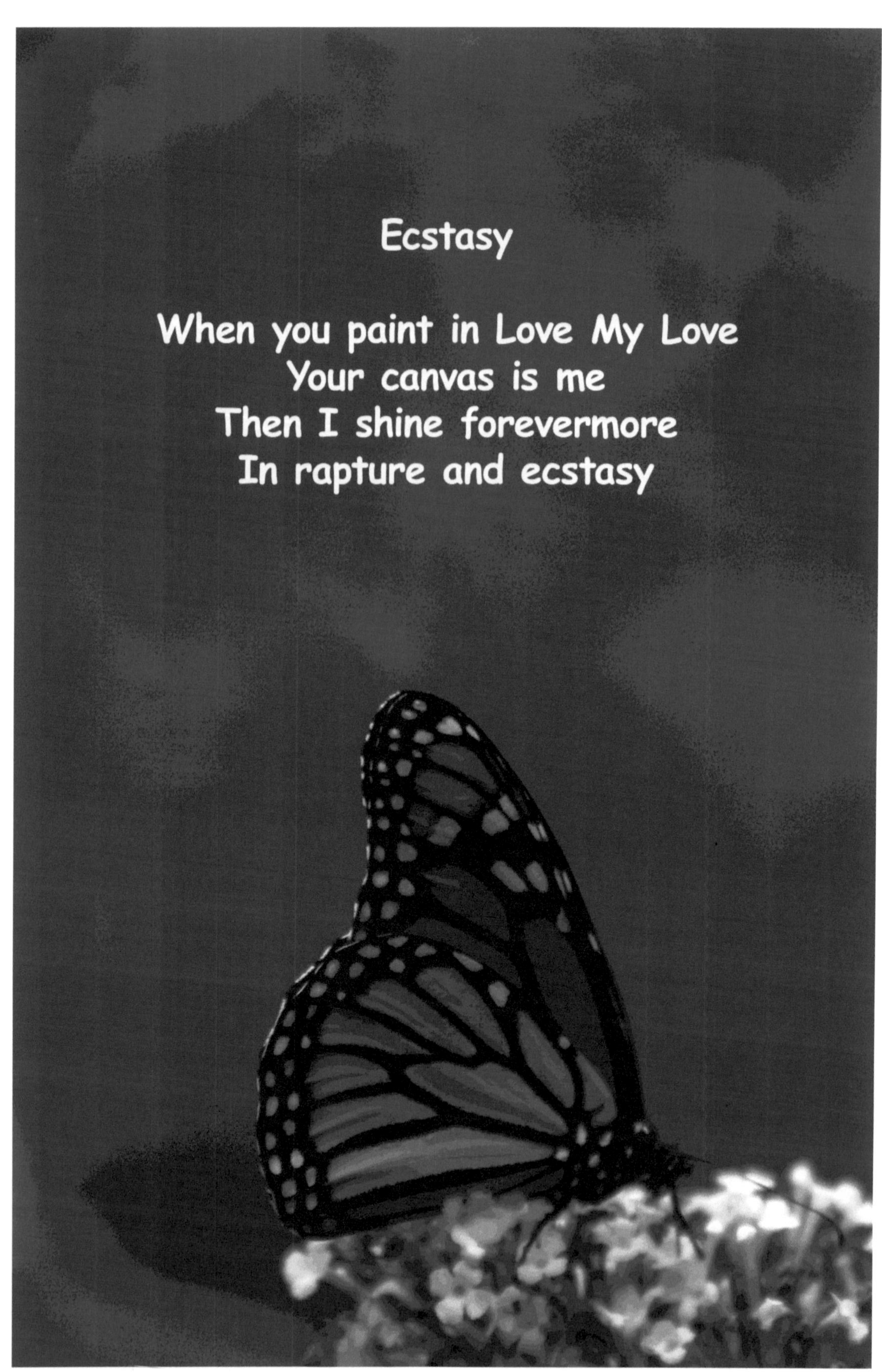
Ecstasy
When you paint in Love My Love
Your canvas is me
Then I shine forevermore
In rapture and ecstasy

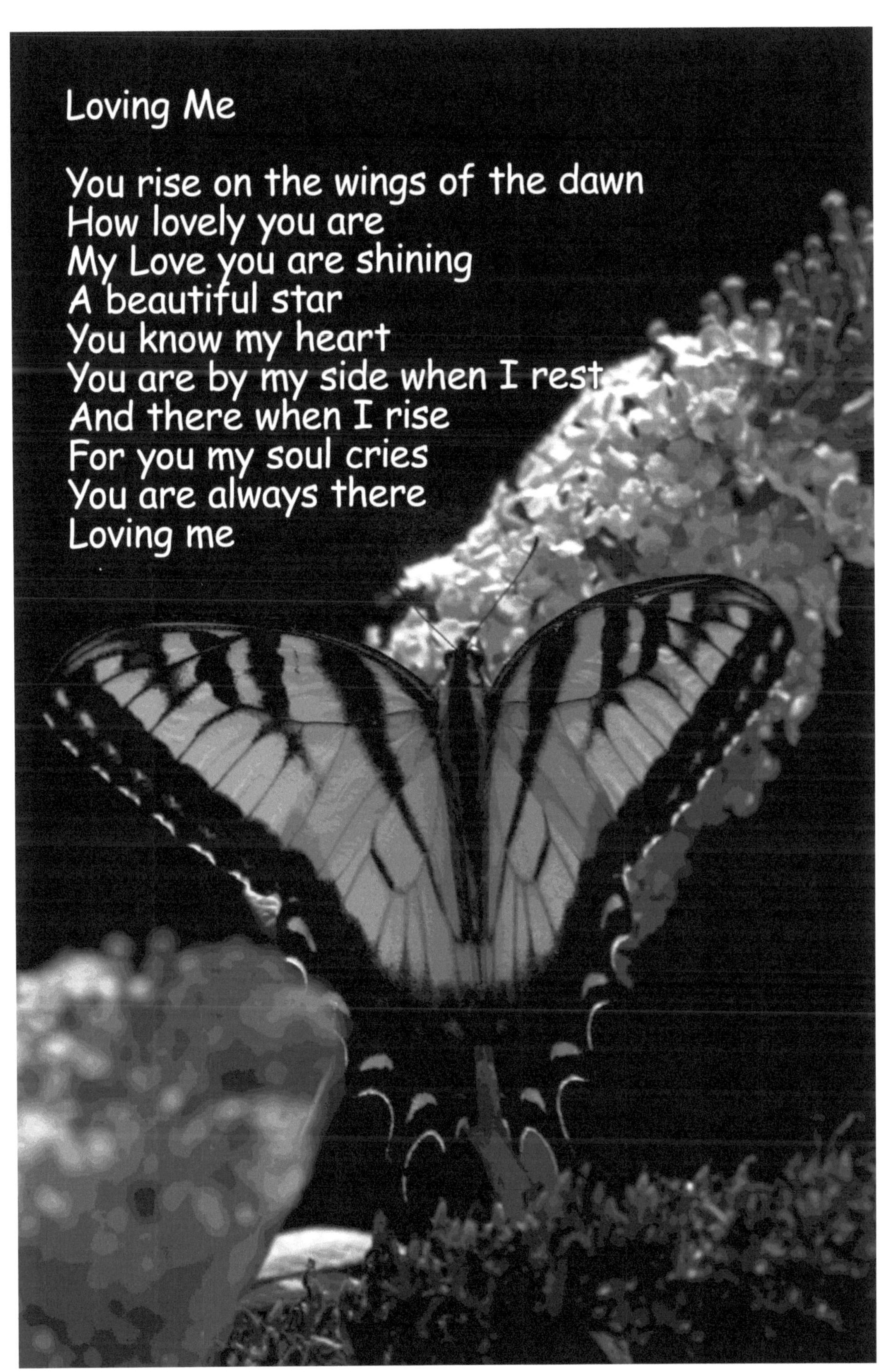
Loving Me
You rise on the wings of the dawn
How lovely you are
My Love you are shining
A beautiful star
You know my heart
You are by my side when I rest
And there when I rise
For you my soul cries
You are always there
Loving me

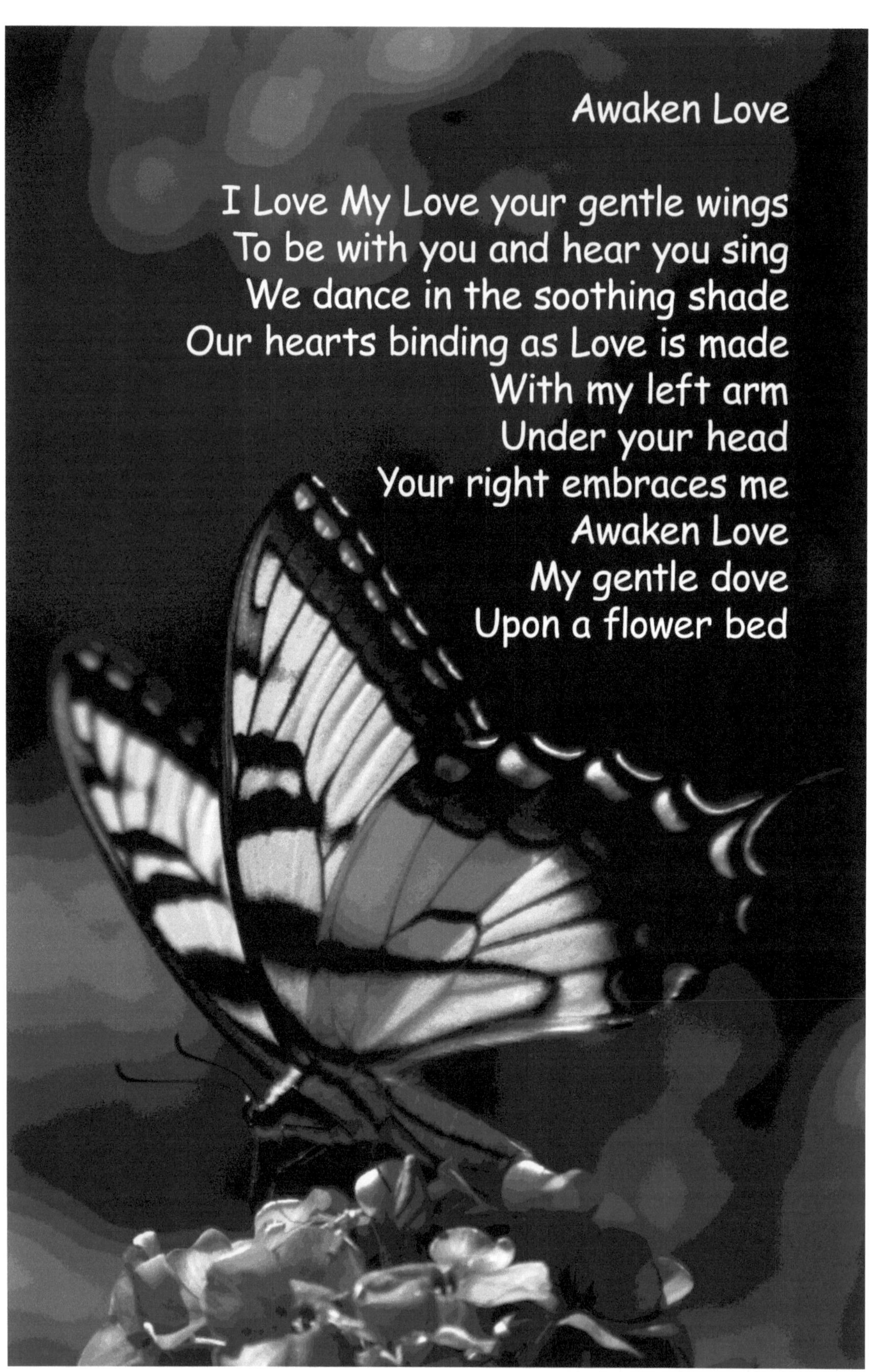
Awaken Love
I Love My Love your gentle wings
To be with you and hear you sing
We dance in the soothing shade
Our hearts binding as Love is made
With my left arm
Under your head
Your right embraces me
Awaken Love
My gentle dove
Upon a flower bed

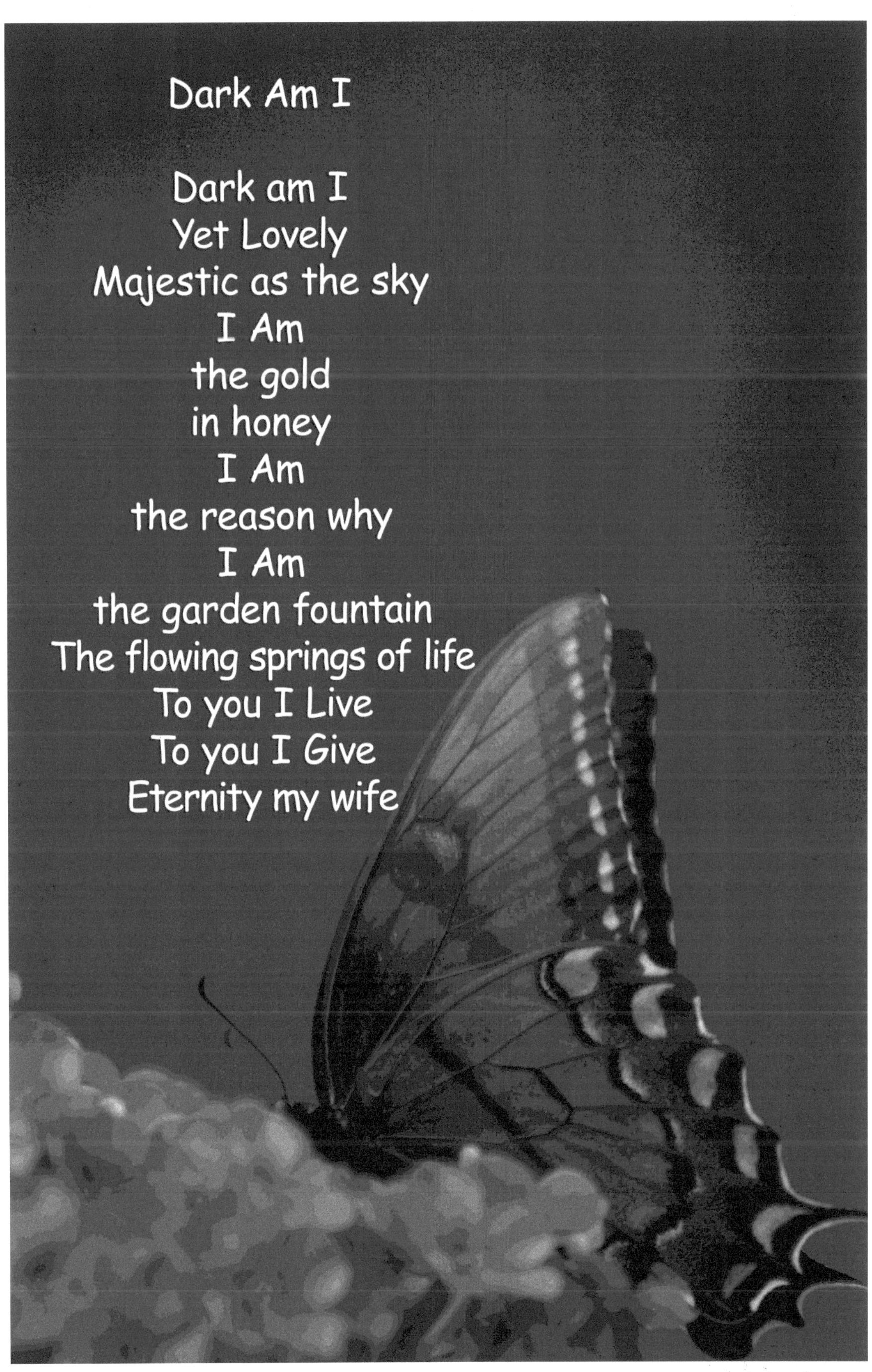
Dark Am I

Dark am I
Yet Lovely
Majestic as the sky
I Am
the gold
in honey
I Am
the reason why
I Am
the garden fountain
The flowing springs of life
To you I Live
To you I Give
Eternity my wife

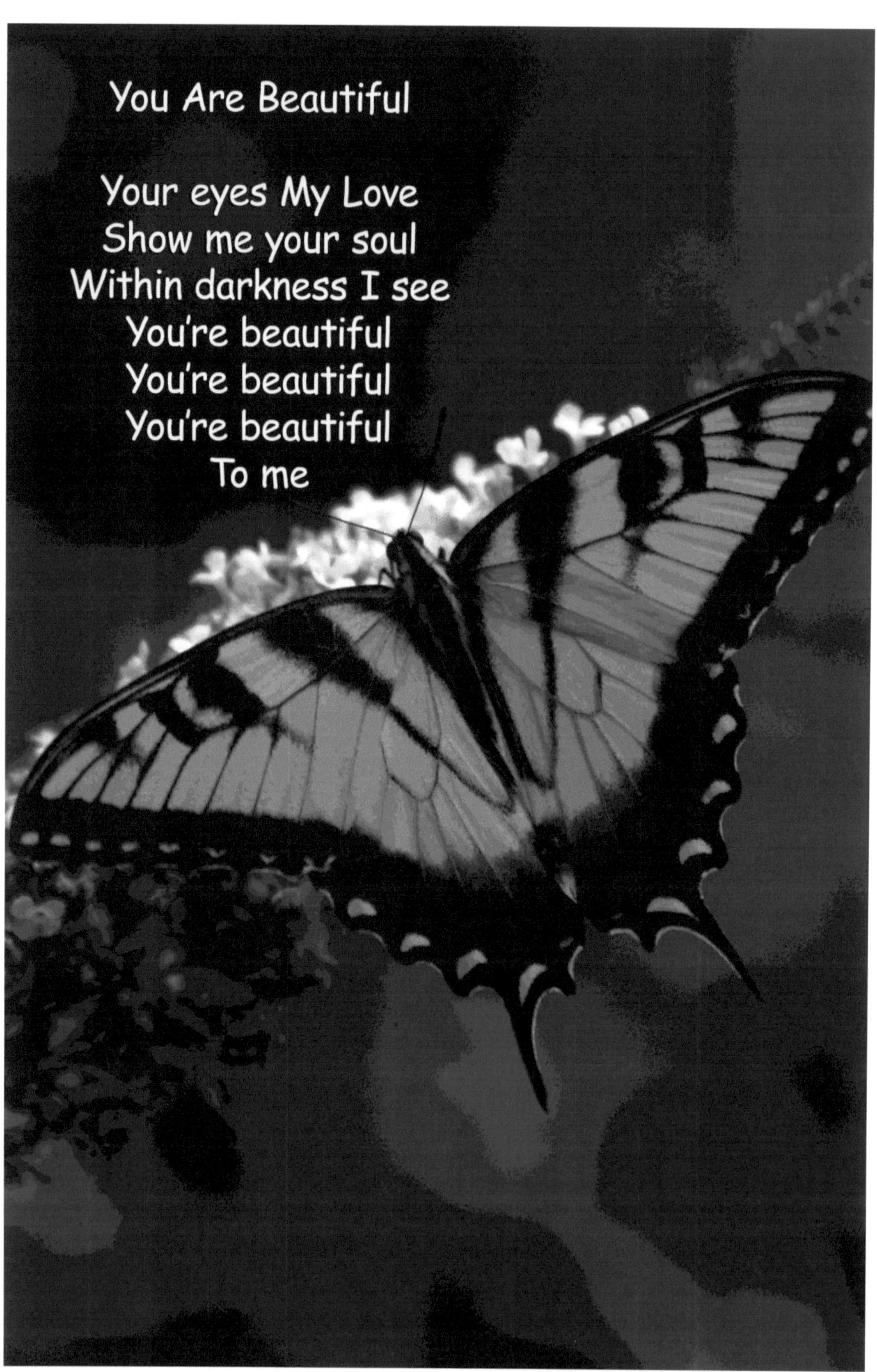
You Are Beautiful

Your eyes My Love
Show me your soul
Within darkness I see
You're beautiful
You're beautiful
You're beautiful
To me

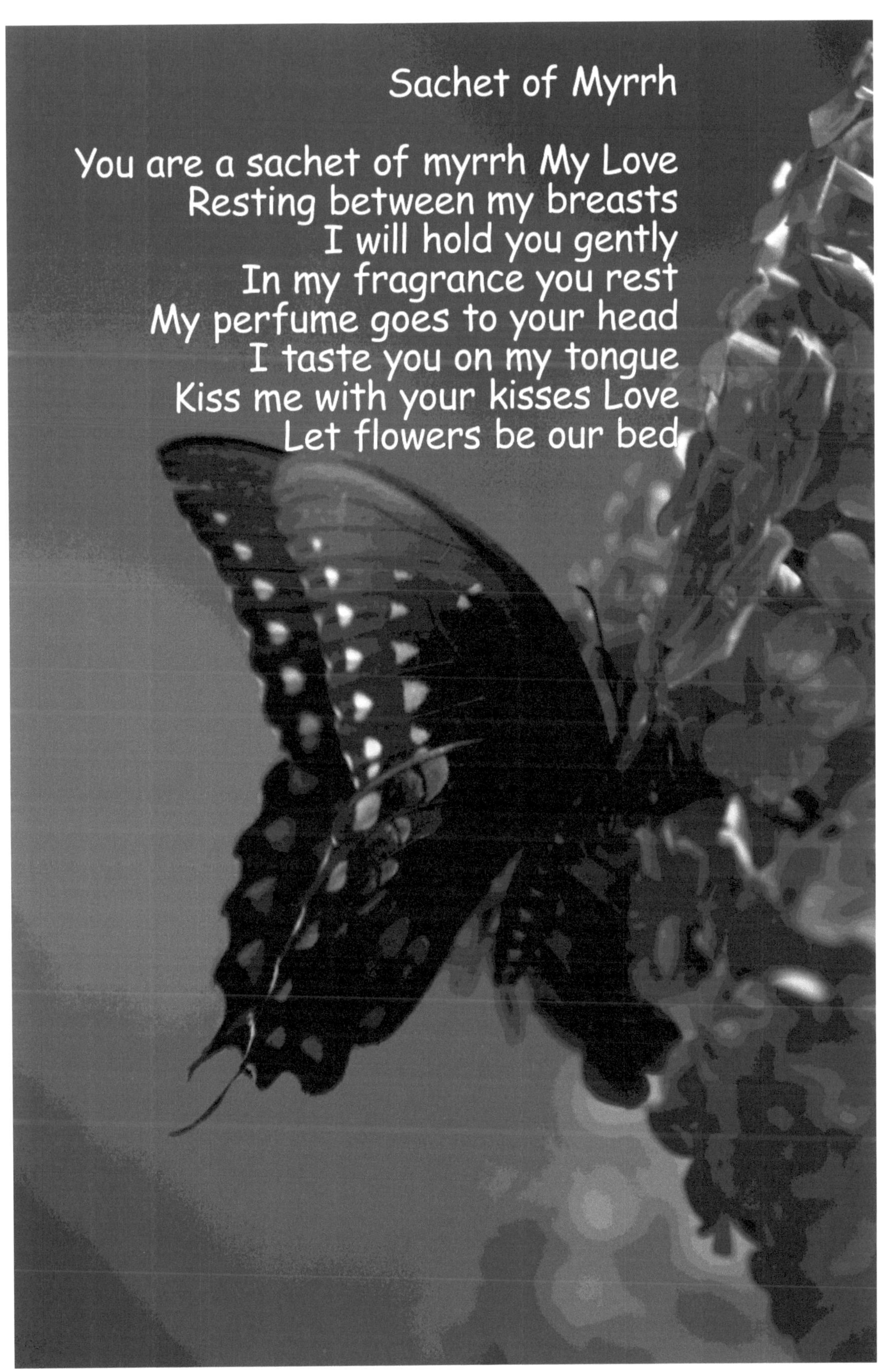
Sachet of Myrrh
You are a sachet of myrrh My Love
Resting between my breasts
I will hold you gently
In my fragrance you rest
My perfume goes to your head
I taste you on my tongue
Kiss me with your kisses Love
Let flowers be our bed

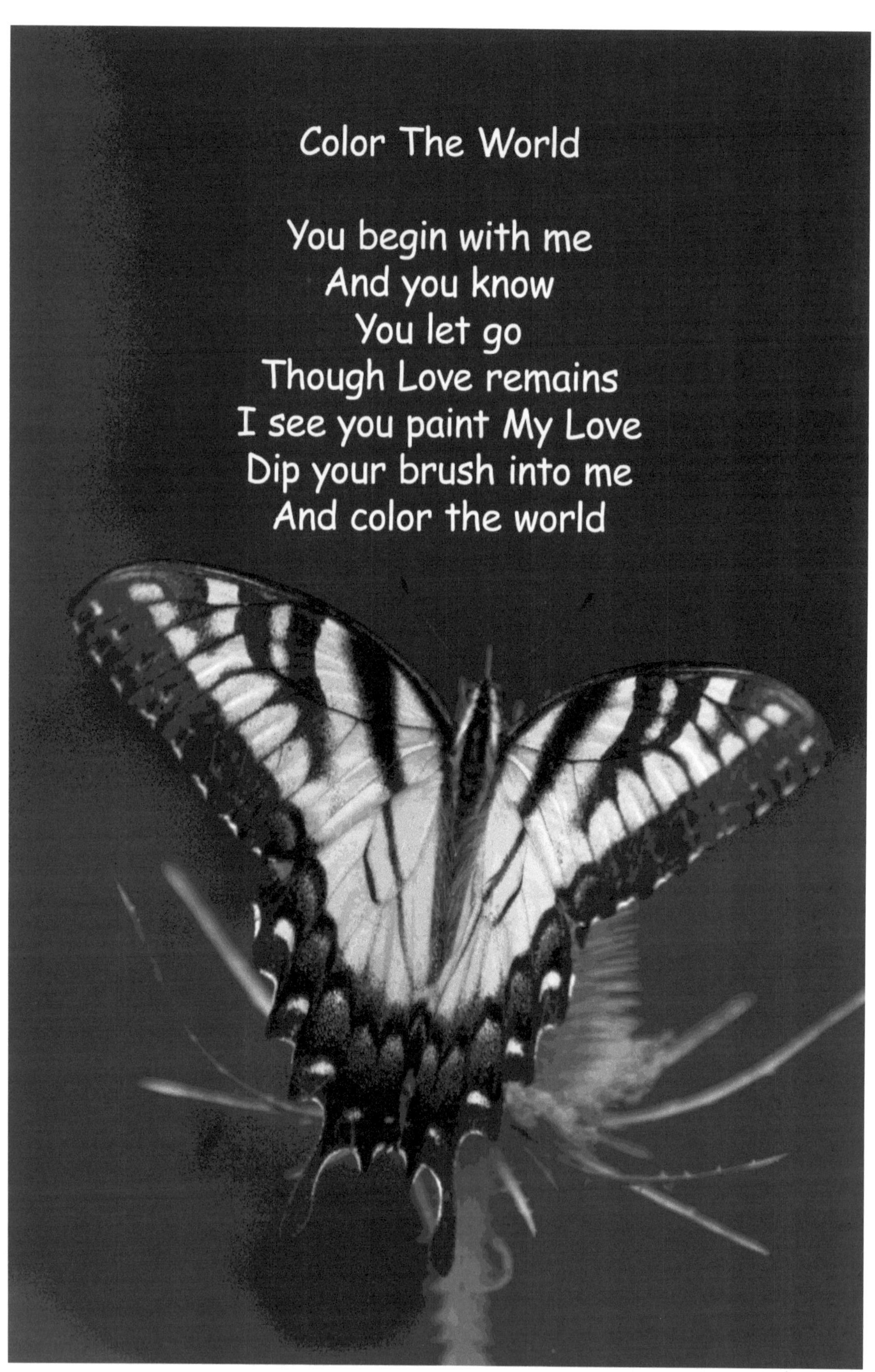
Color The World

You begin with me
And you know
You let go
Though Love remains
I see you paint My Love
Dip your brush into me
And color the world

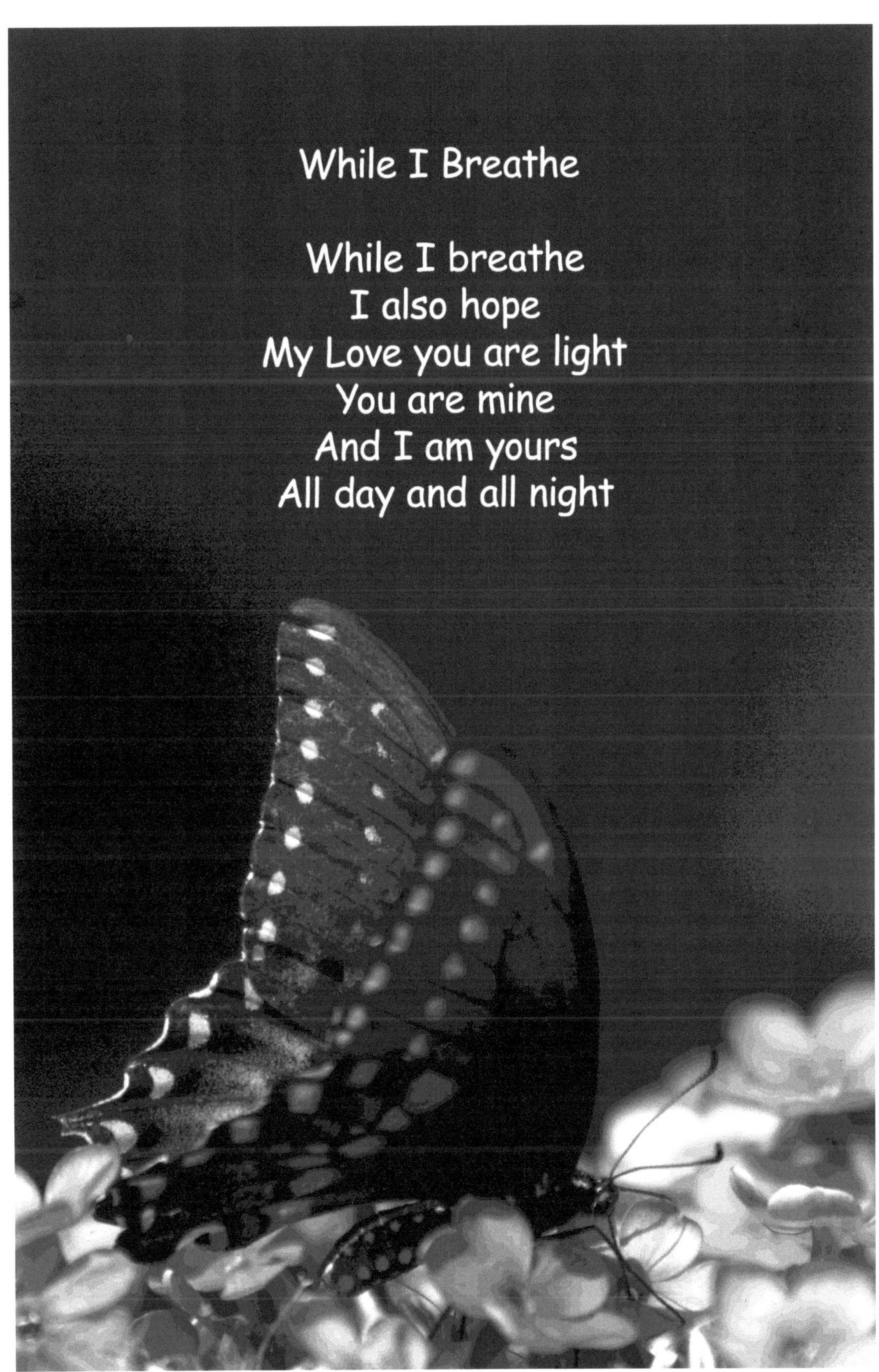
While I Breathe

While I breathe
I also hope
My Love you are light
You are mine
And I am yours
All day and all night

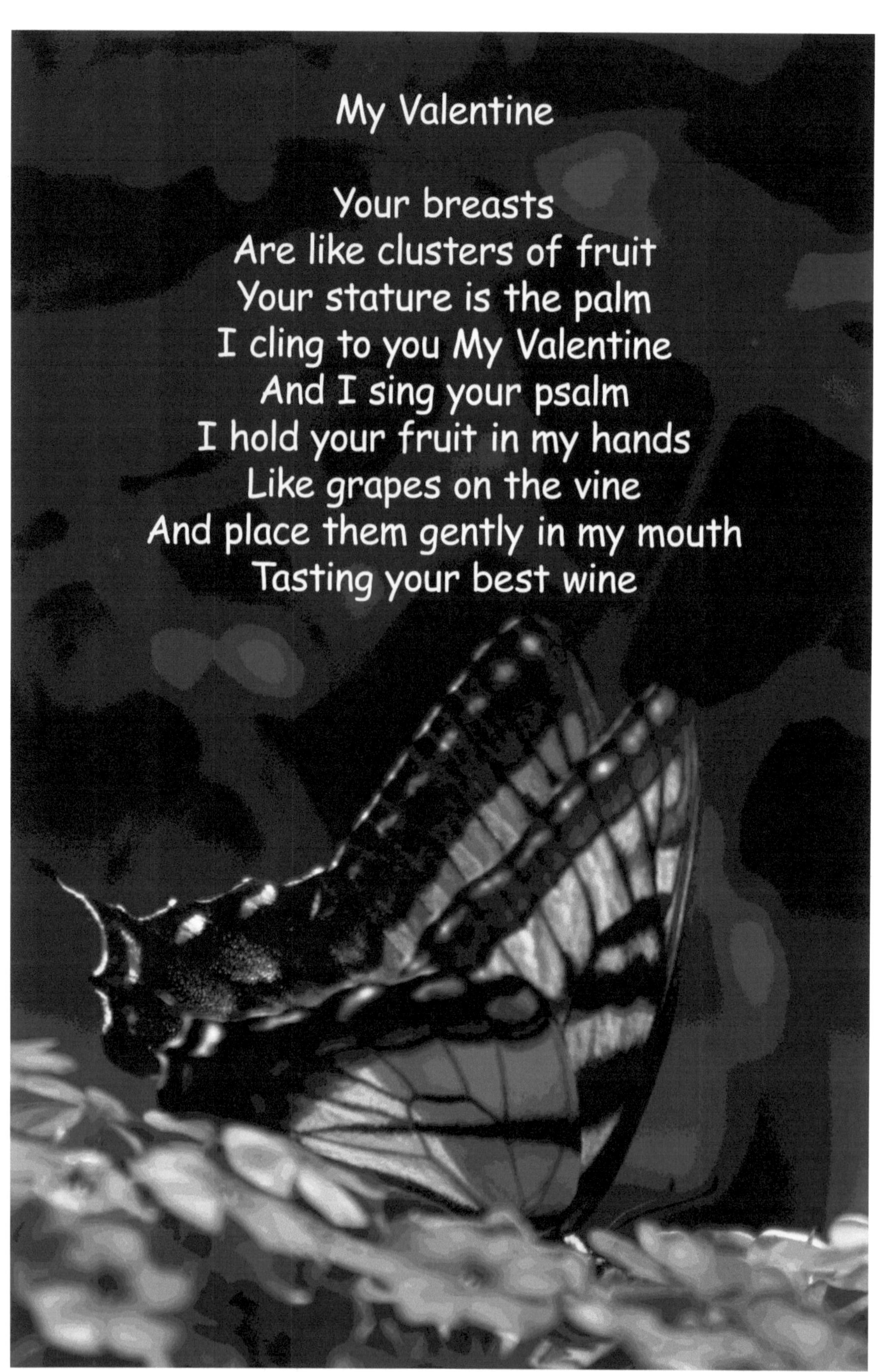
My Valentine
Your breasts
Are like clusters of fruit
Your stature is the palm
I cling to you My Valentine
And I sing your psalm
I hold your fruit in my hands
Like grapes on the vine
And place them gently in my mouth
Tasting your best wine

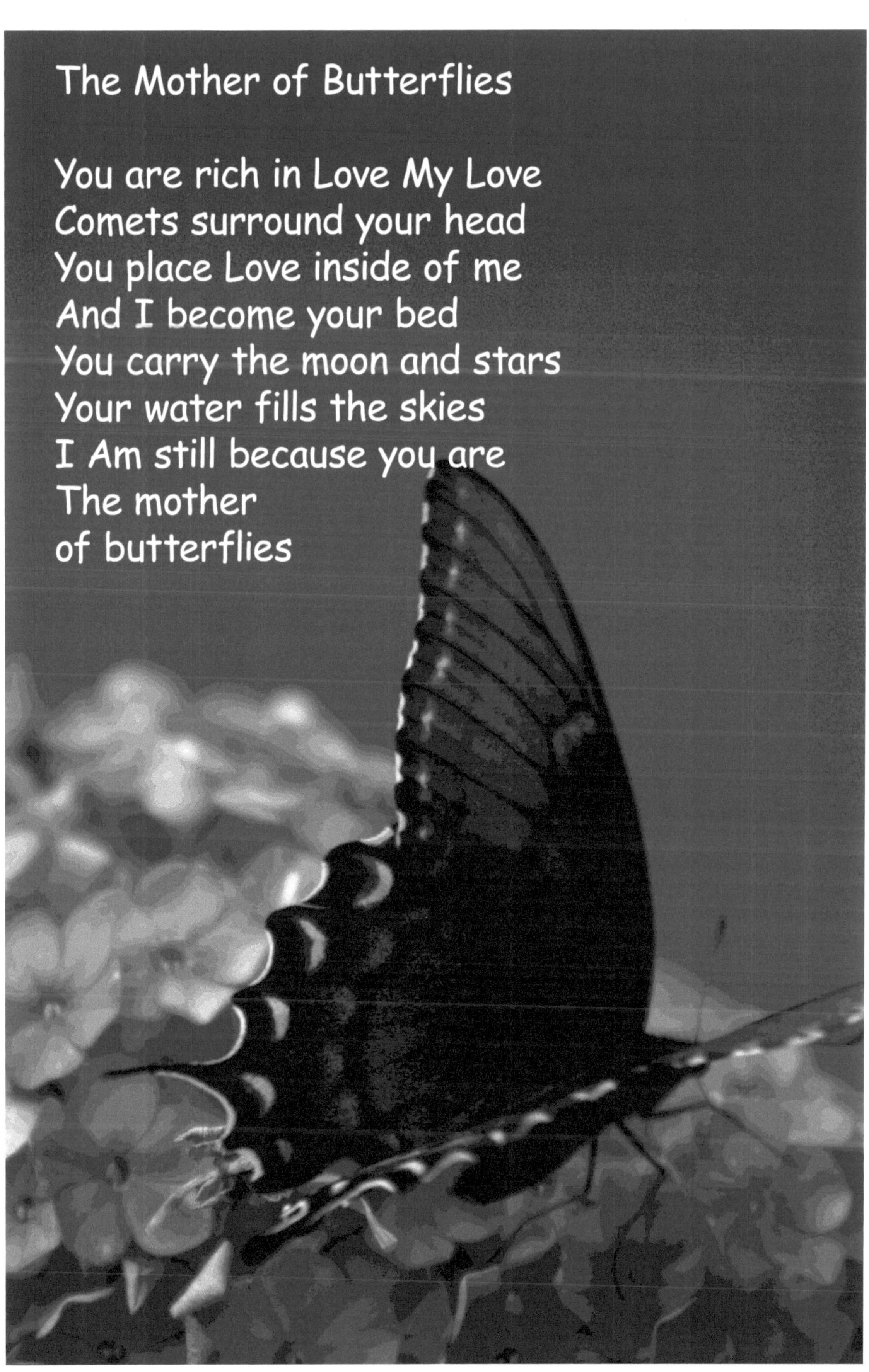
The Mother of Butterflies

You are rich in Love My Love
Comets surround your head
You place Love inside of me
And I become your bed
You carry the moon and stars
Your water fills the skies
I Am still because you are
The mother
of butterflies

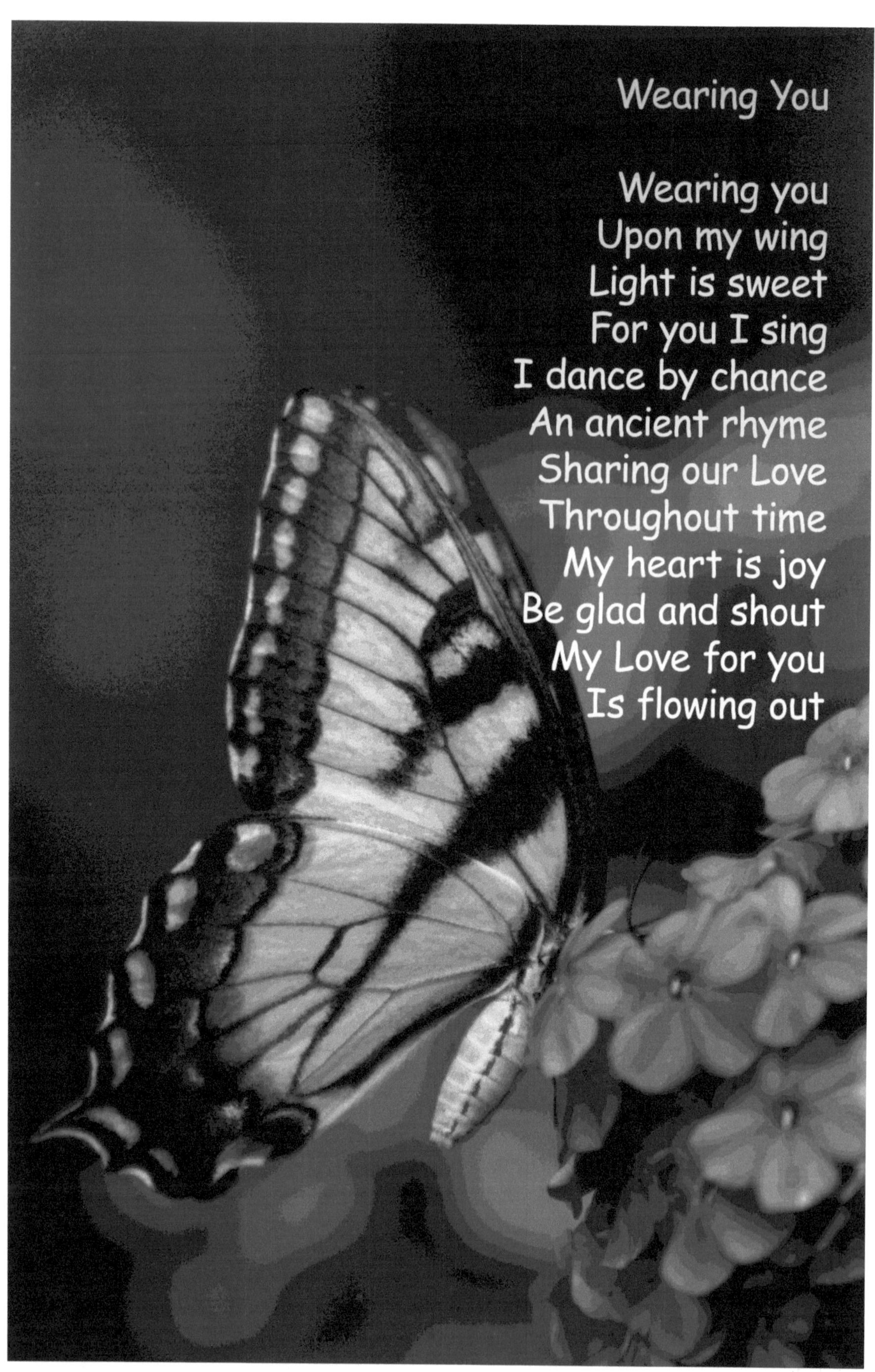
Wearing You

Wearing you
Upon my wing
Light is sweet
For you I sing
I dance by chance
An ancient rhyme
Sharing our Love
Throughout time
My heart is joy
Be glad and shout
My Love for you
Is flowing out

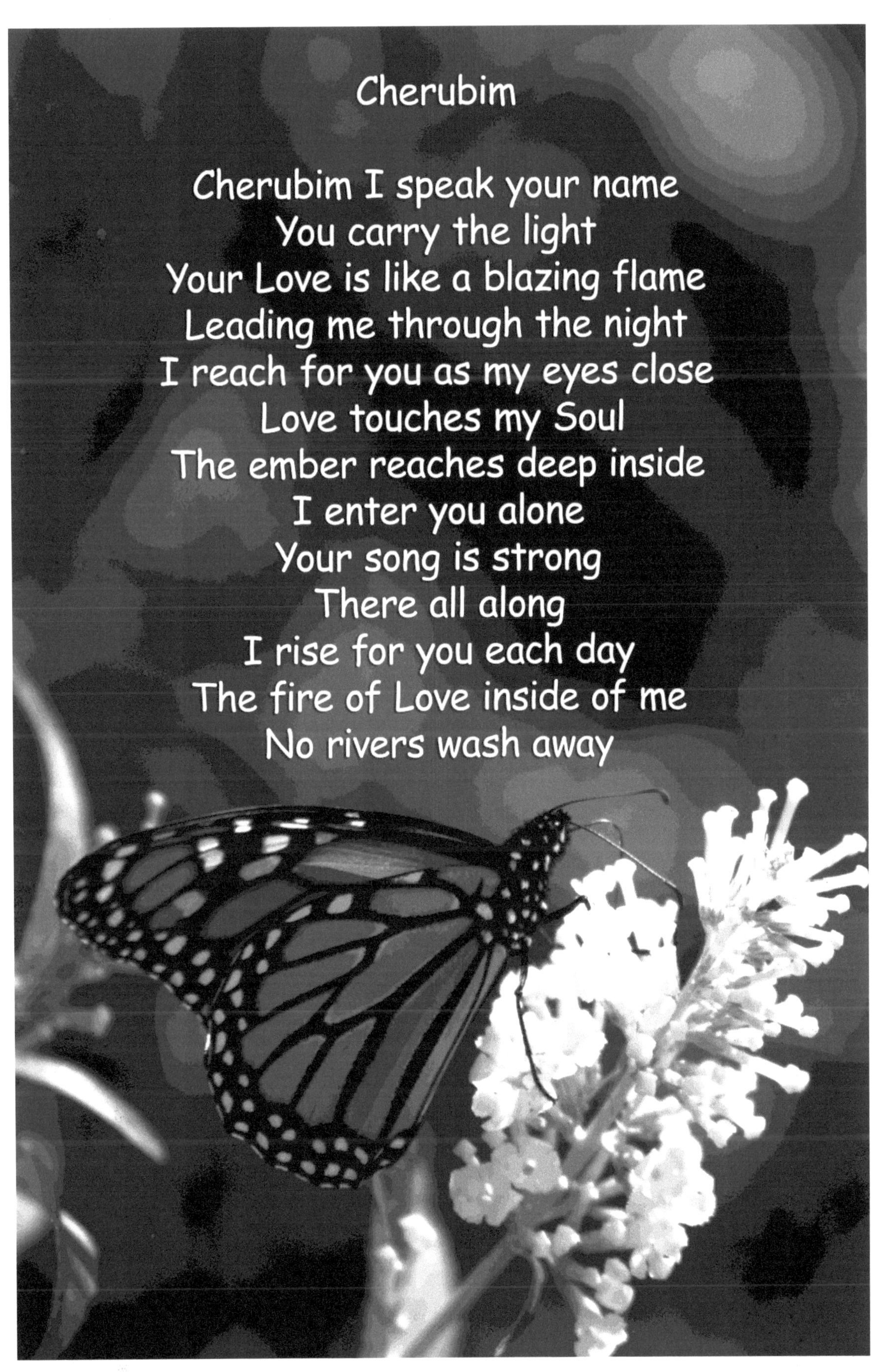
Cherubim

Cherubim I speak your name
You carry the light
Your Love is like a blazing flame
Leading me through the night
I reach for you as my eyes close
Love touches my Soul
The ember reaches deep inside
I enter you alone
Your song is strong
There all along
I rise for you each day
The fire of Love inside of me
No rivers wash away

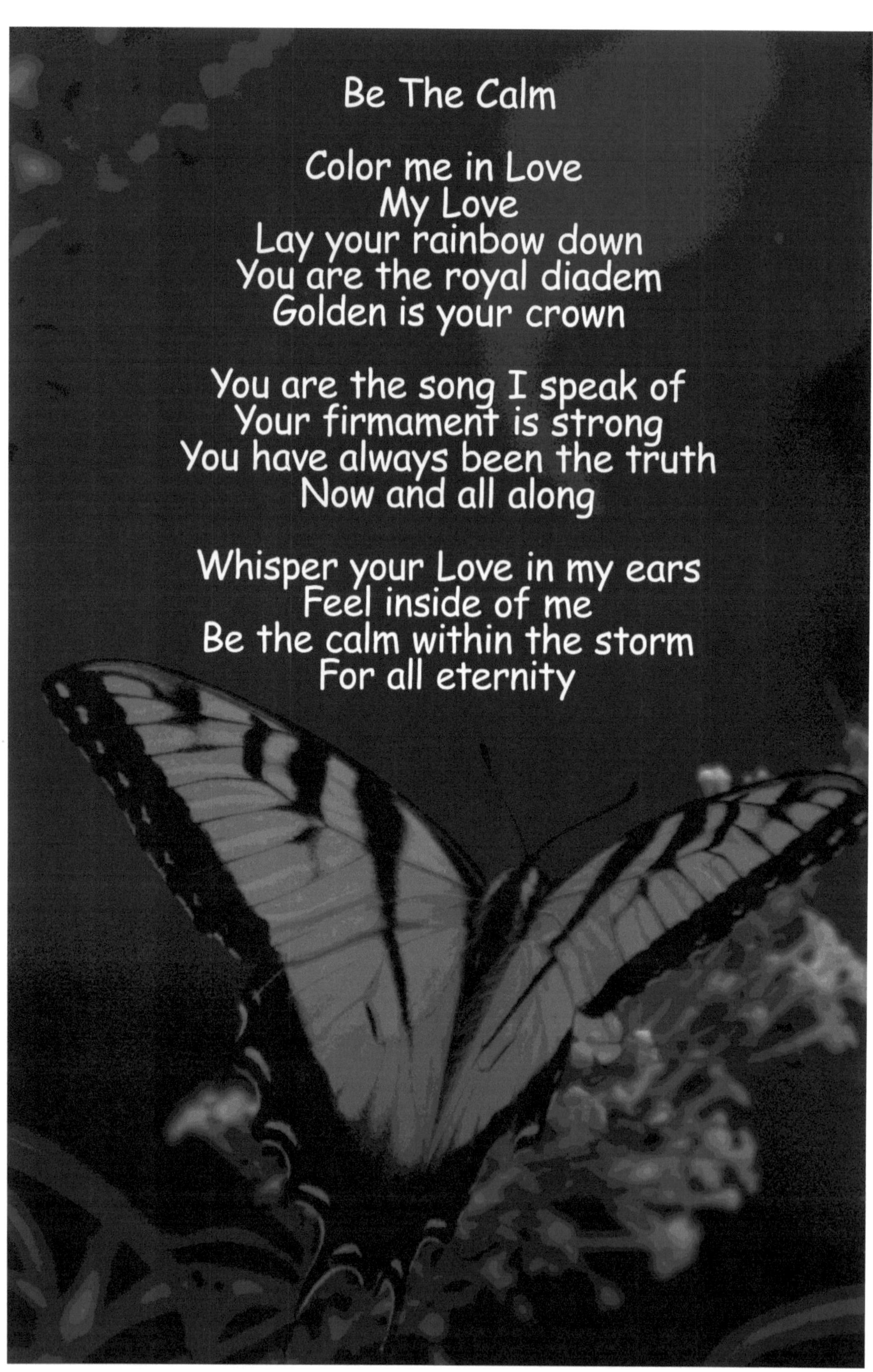
Be The Calm

Color me in Love
My Love
Lay your rainbow down
You are the royal diadem
Golden is your crown

You are the song I speak of
Your firmament is strong
You have always been the truth
Now and all along

Whisper your Love in my ears
Feel inside of me
Be the calm within the storm
For all eternity

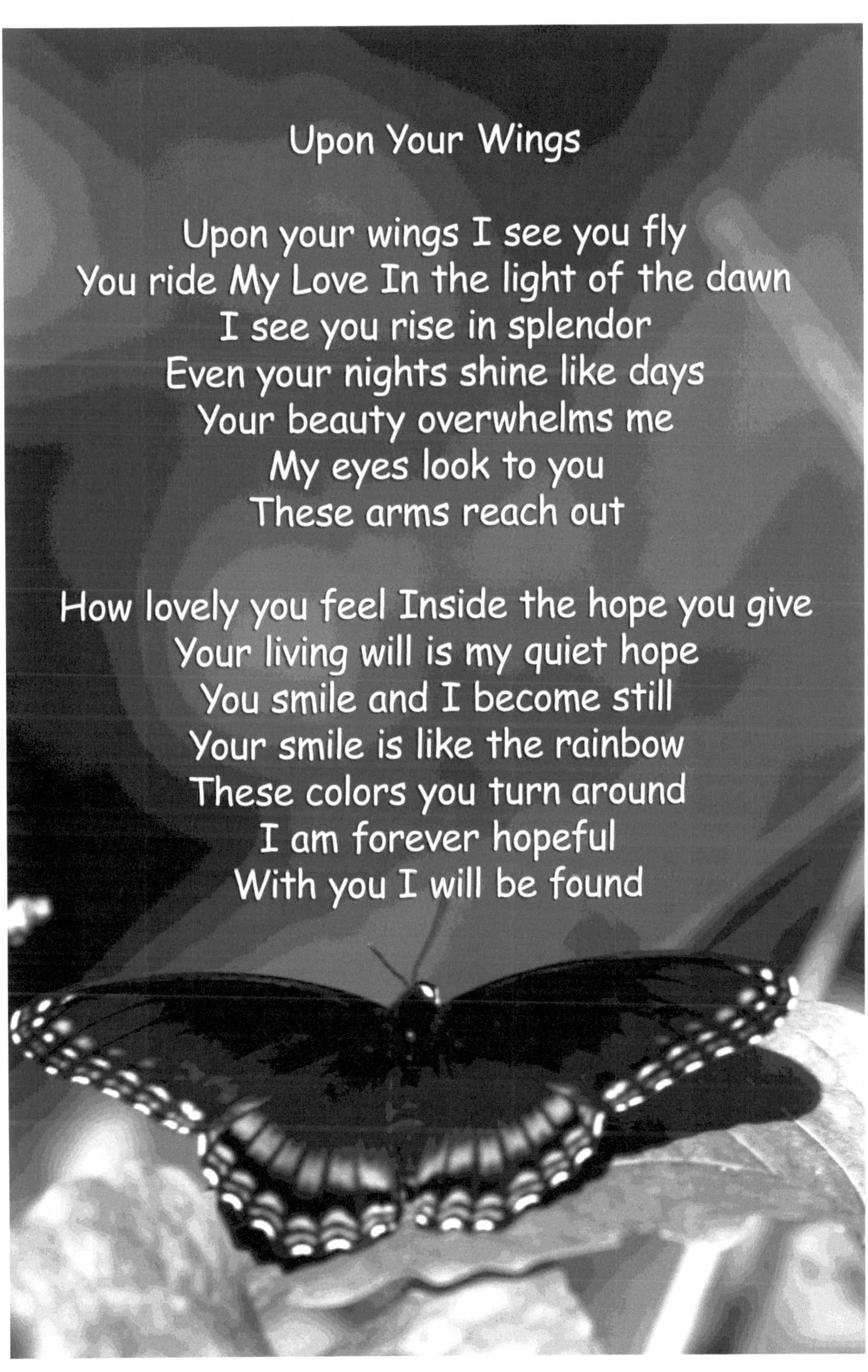

Upon Your Wings

Upon your wings I see you fly
You ride My Love In the light of the dawn
I see you rise in splendor
Even your nights shine like days
Your beauty overwhelms me
My eyes look to you
These arms reach out

How lovely you feel Inside the hope you give
Your living will is my quiet hope
You smile and I become still
Your smile is like the rainbow
These colors you turn around
I am forever hopeful
With you I will be found

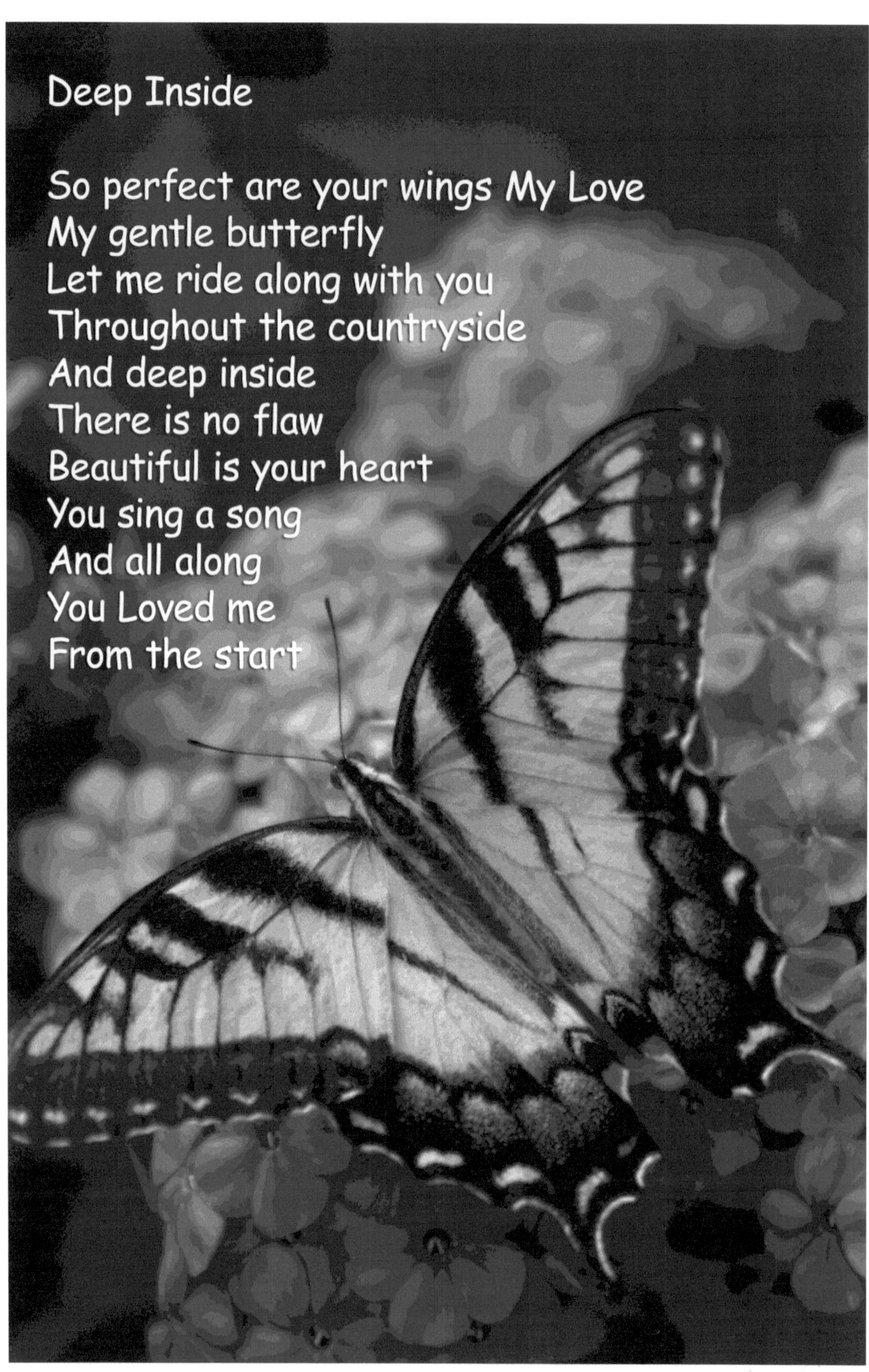
Deep Inside

So perfect are your wings My Love
My gentle butterfly
Let me ride along with you
Throughout the countryside
And deep inside
There is no flaw
Beautiful is your heart
You sing a song
And all along
You Loved me
From the start

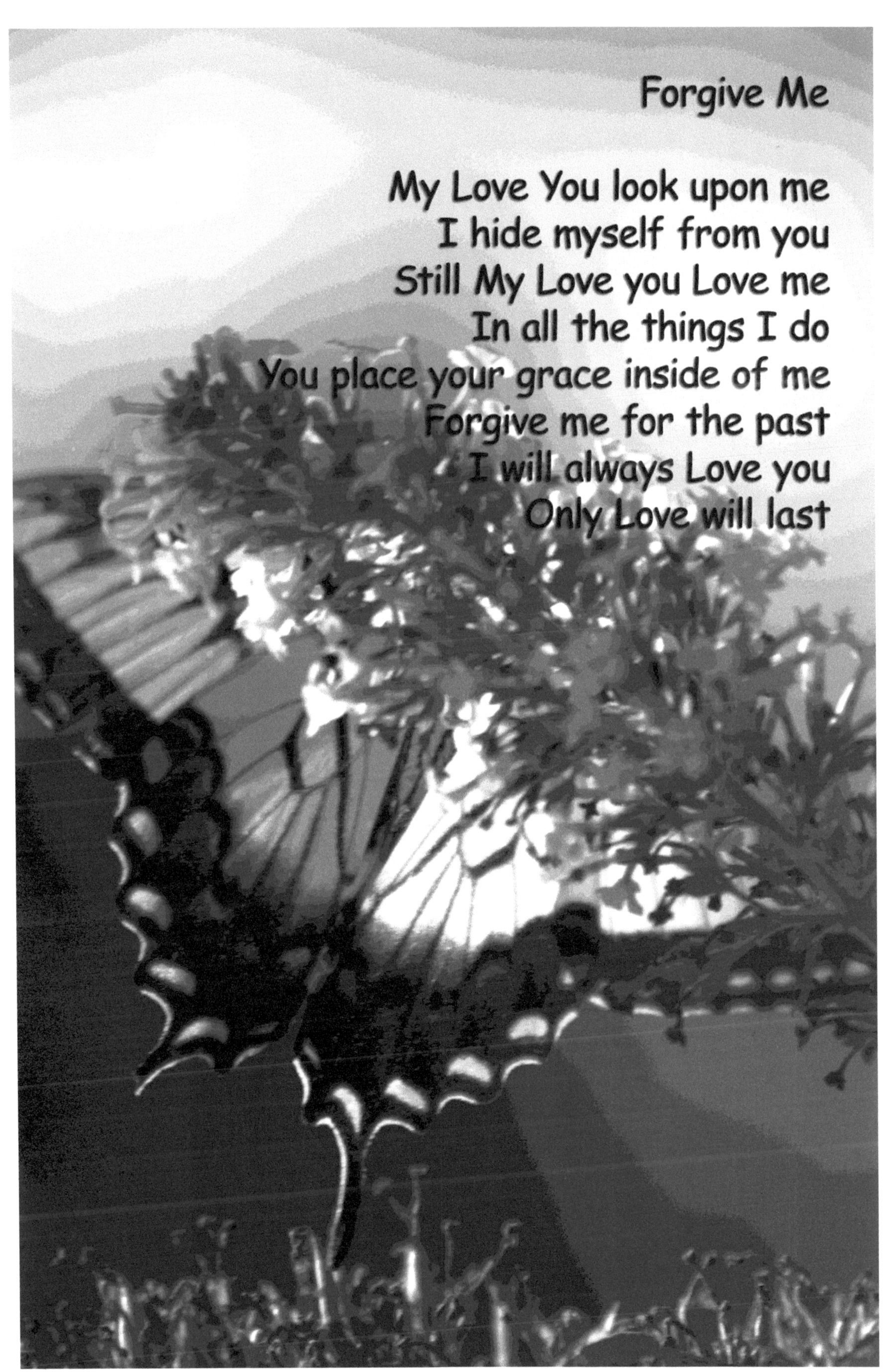
Forgive Me

My Love You look upon me
I hide myself from you
Still My Love you Love me
In all the things I do
You place your grace inside of me
Forgive me for the past
I will always Love you
Only Love will last

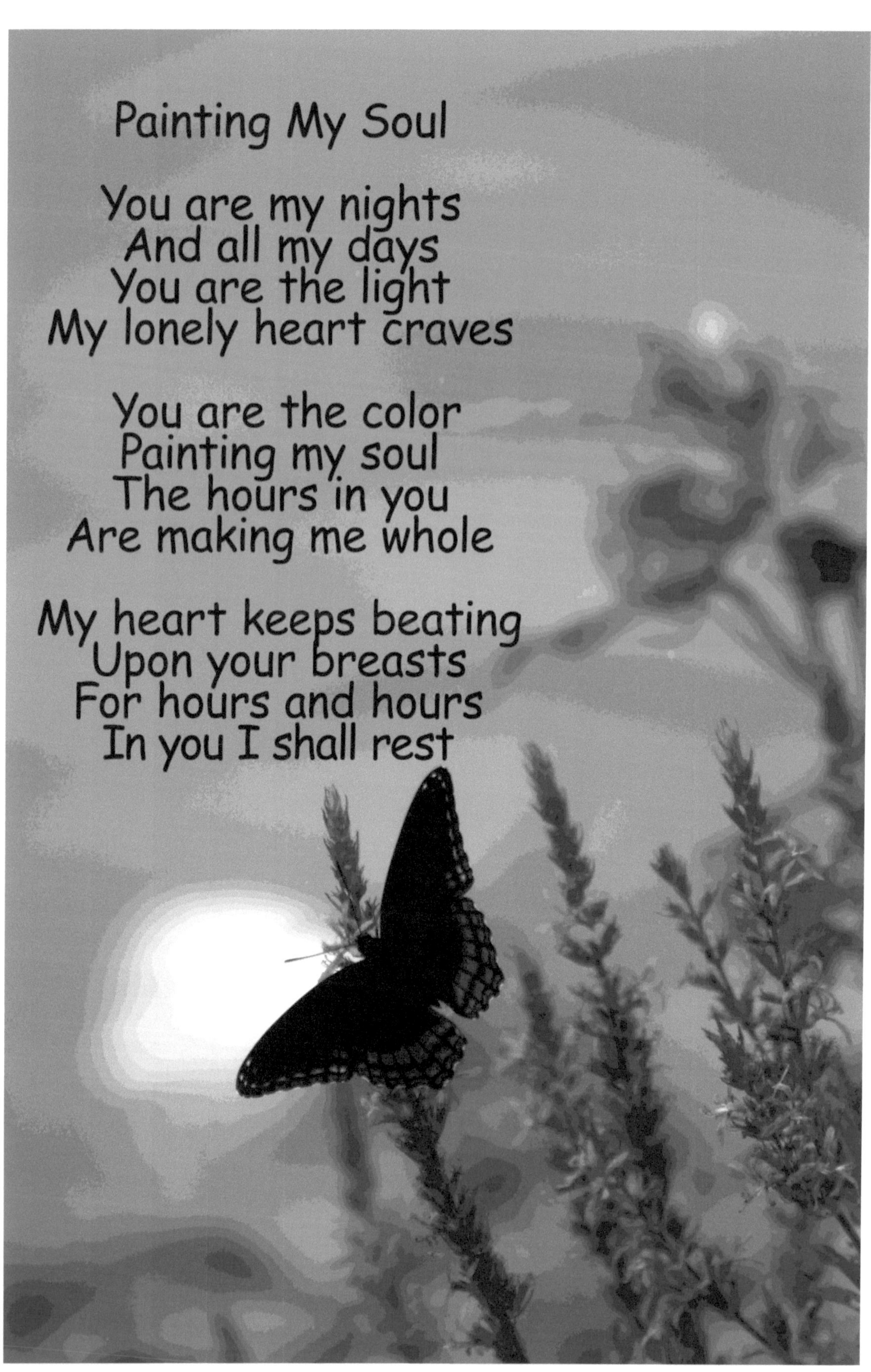

Painting My Soul

You are my nights
And all my days
You are the light
My lonely heart craves

You are the color
Painting my soul
The hours in you
Are making me whole

My heart keeps beating
Upon your breasts
For hours and hours
In you I shall rest

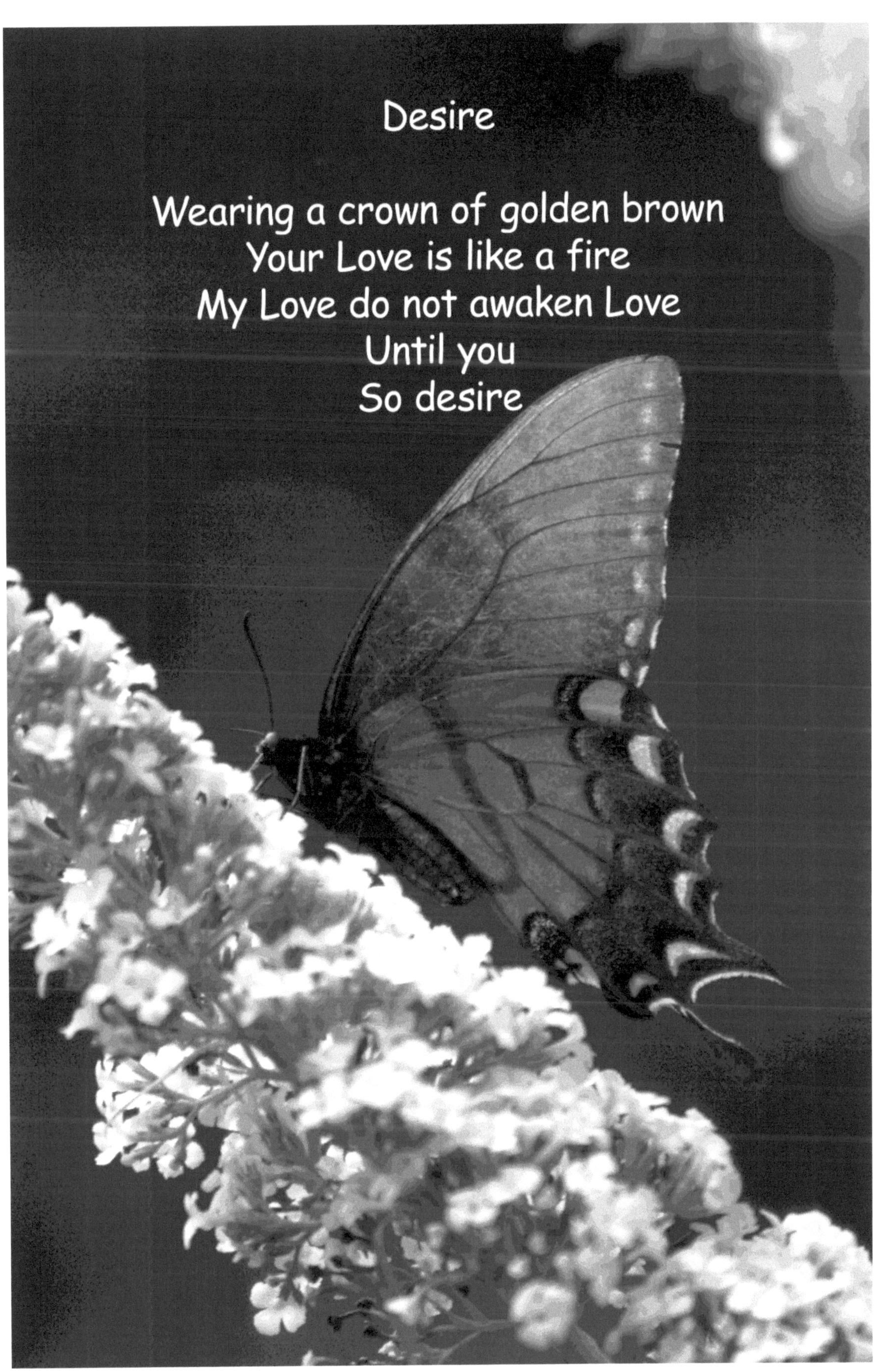
Desire
Wearing a crown of golden brown
Your Love is like a fire
My Love do not awaken Love
Until you
So desire

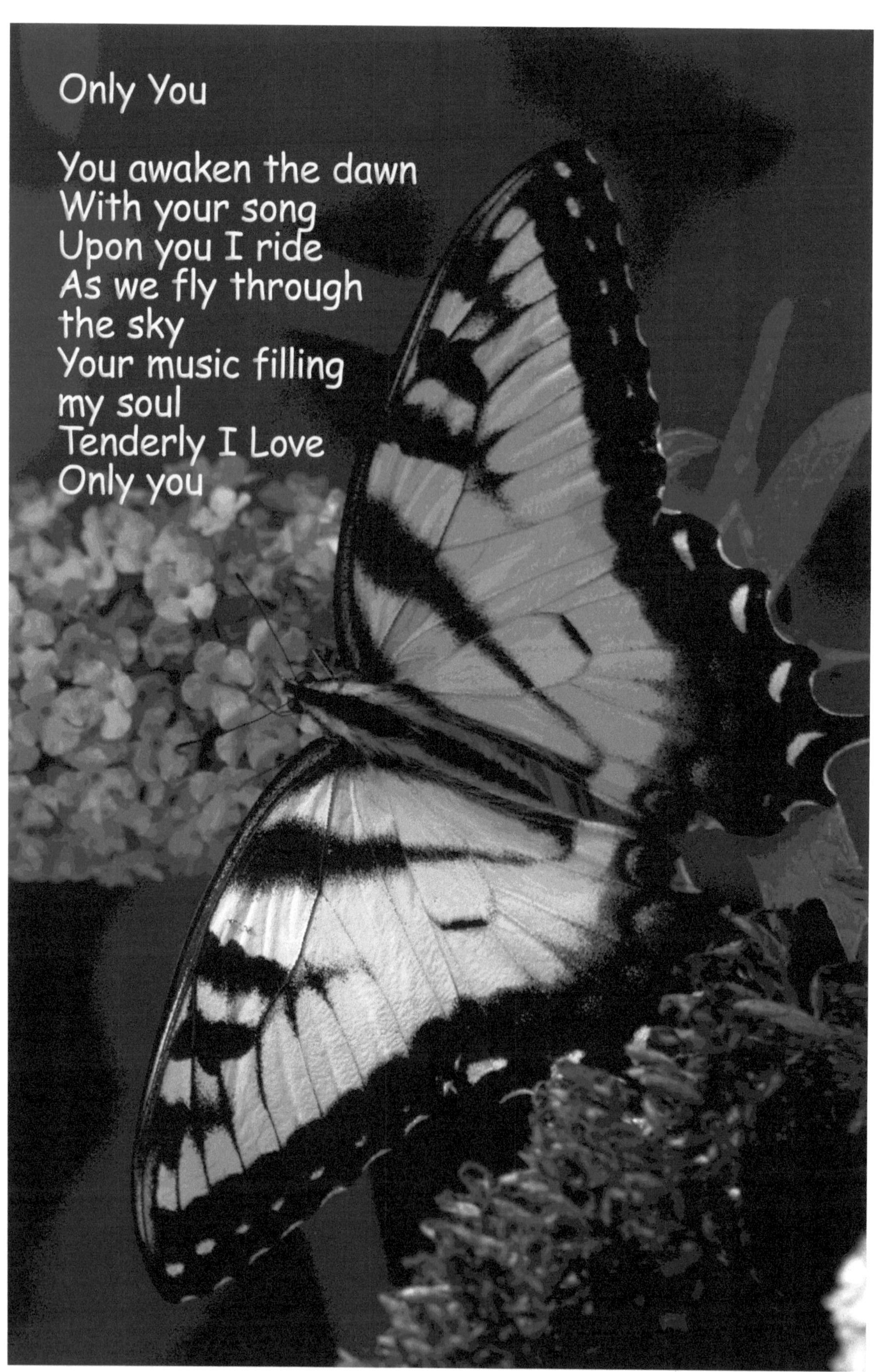
Only You

You awaken the dawn
With your song
Upon you I ride
As we fly through
the sky
Your music filling
my soul
Tenderly I Love
Only you

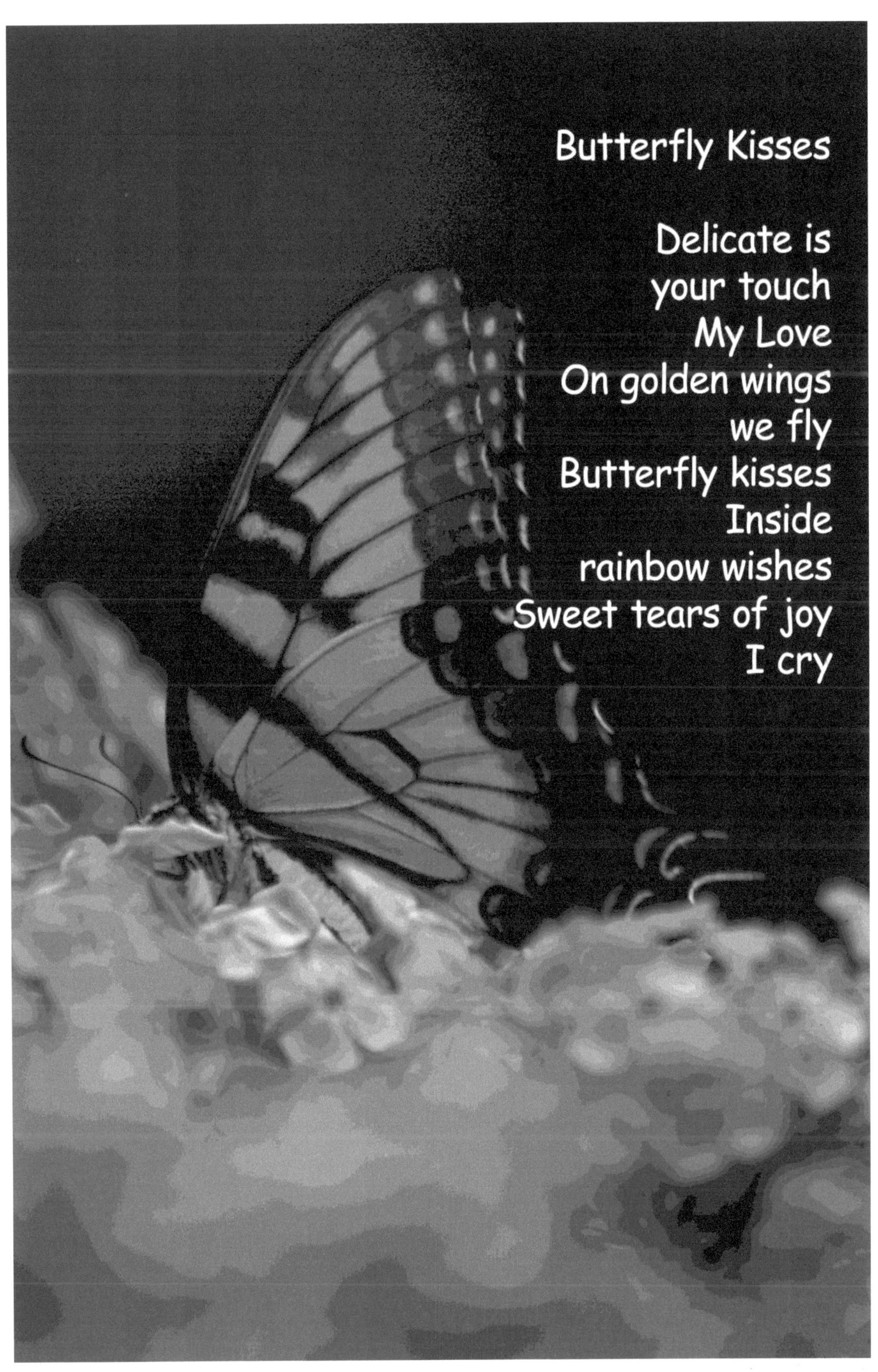
Butterfly Kisses
Delicate is
your touch
My Love
On golden wings
we fly
Butterfly kisses
Inside
rainbow wishes
Sweet tears of joy
I cry

Dr. Claus combines his love of poetry, photography,
and nature to create art.
His published works include:

A Gift of Love
Parsifal
Love Poems 101
To Thee I Sing
Poems Of Love
The Promise
Daughter Of Kings
When You Breathe
My Love Whispers
The Poetess
Inhale Deeply
My Lover
Clair de Lune Serenade
My Gentle Butterfly
The Poetess (Aquarelle)
The Poetess (Luz Celestial)
The Promise (Aquarelle)
The Promise (Luz Celestial)
My Lover (Aquarelle)
To Thee I Sing (Aquarelle)
To Thee I Sing (Luz Celestial)
Inhale Deeply (Aquarelle)
Inhale Deeply (Luz Celestial)
The Keeper Of The Stones
My Love Whispers (Aquarelle)
My Love Whispers (Luz Celestial)
When You Breathe (Aquarelle)
Daughter Of Kings (Aquarelle)
Medley Mole Meets Buddy Rabbit
The Light Of The Trees El Corazon
Crumble Rumble Stumble Stew
Chuck Hug A Lunkle Ching Choo - Choo
A Hairy Scary Spider

www.ingramcontent.com/pod-product-compliance
Lightning Source LLC
LaVergne TN
LVHW070204110826
845147LV00002B/500

9781614970149